PERFORMANCE

using performance for substance abuse prevention

United Nations Office
for Drug Control
and Crime Prevention

Global
Youth
Network

United Nations publication

Sales No. E.03.XI.7

ISBN 92-1-148158-9

TABLE OF CONTENTS

INTRODUCTION

Using Performance for Drug Abuse Prevention

The Global Youth Network project was started by the UNDCP in 1998 with a view to giving young people their rightful place in the scheme of things. The idea was to allow young people to have a say in designing and implementing drug abuse prevention projects so that their legitimate knowledge of issues surrounding youth culture could be effectively used to prevent substance abuse.

As part of the project a meeting of youth groups that use performance to combat drug abuse was organized in Puebla, Mexico, from the 11th to the 15th of September, 2000. The aim of the meeting was to synthesize the experiences of the youth groups in order to create a set of guidelines for other youth groups or youth workers who might want to start programmes based on performance or to include performance in on-going programmes.

The guidelines included in this publication aim to create a framework of basic principles, requirements and skills needed to use performance as an effective tool for drug abuse prevention. They do not delve into the organizational minutiae of planning and executing a project which are covered in the handbook for new youth groups that is also being produced by the UNDCP. We include testimonials from youth who are part of substance abuse prevention programmes as also some practical tips for creating exciting new projects. These guidelines are meant to be used in conjunction with other detailed materials produced by UN organizations and other organizations across the world, some of which are cited herein.

It bears repetition that these guiding principles originate from youth. They are a culmination of the practical experiences of all the youth groups involved with the global youth network against drug abuse and especially of the groups that attended the Puebla meeting.

We would like to acknowledge the contribution of Ms Jan Taylor, performance expert with the Alberta Alcohol and Drug Abuse Commission, Canada who structured and conducted the meeting in Puebla and helped formulate and write these guidelines.

Hands-on meeting on the use of performance for drug abuse prevention

Puebla, Mexico, September 11th to 15th, 2000

NAME OF GROUP	ADDRESS/CONTACT	NAMES OF MEETING ATTENDEES
Angaza	PO BOX 35451, Nairobi, Kenya E-mail: angazalife@hotmail.com	Raymond Kiruki Joy Kiruki Onyari Bikundo
All Stars Talent Show	Network 500, Greenwich Street # 201 New York, NY 10013 Tel: +1 (212) 941-9400 E-mail: astsn@aol.com	Pam Lewis Antoine Joyce Bryant Pabon
Organizacion De Jovenes Revolucionarios, Mexico	4. Cerrada De Fresno M7 L 15 Colonia Agranista Iztapalapa, CP 09760, Mexico DF Tel: 54285699	Rafael G. Martinez Marco A. Jimenez
Eventos X Amor	Manzana "K", Lote 16, Residenciales, Nimajay Z. 7, Mixco, Guatemala E-mail: eventosxamor@latinmail.com	Silvia Espinoza
Lo Que Sea? (UCPI)	Calle 13#3-07, Bogota, Colombia E-mail: pgrajales@yahoo.com	Ada Rodriguez Arlex Barajas Marcello Cantillo
XIBALBA	Residencial Granada, Bloque J"28", Casa #1106 Tegucicalpa, Honduras, C.A. Telefax: 223 0437 E-mail: xibalba@tutopia.com	Wanndha Pavon
STEP	A1/82 Hastal Road, Uttam Nagar, New Delhi, India, Tel: 91 11 5626667, E-mail: rockylalima@usa.net, rockylalima@yahoo.com	Rakesh Bhardwaj Lalima Singh
UNDCP Regional Office for Mexico and Central America	Presidente Mazryk, No 29, Piso 9 Mexico DF Tel: 5 263 9797 E-mail: markus.gottsbacher@un.org.mx Javier.hernandez@un.org.mx Lucero.gudino@un.org.mx	Diana Munoz Markus Gottsbacher Lucero Gudian Javier Hernandez
UNDCP Demand Reduction Section	Vienna International Centre P.O.Box 500, A-1400 Vienna, Austria E-mail: gautam.babbar@undcp.org	Gautam Babbar
AADAC Alberta Alcohol and Drug Abuse Commission – Youth Services	12325 – 140 Street Edmonton, Alberta Canada T5L 2C9 E-mail: jan.taylor@aadac.gov.ab.ca taboo@direct.ca	Jan Taylor

Performance as a Tool to Prevent Substance Abuse

All over the world, young people are involved in and exposed to performance-based group activities that indirectly or directly help prevent substance abuse. They're dancing, singing, clowning and acting, writing, composing and choreographing, producing, designing and exhibiting their work in the most prestigious and the most unexpected spaces, from glitzy theatres in New York to refugee camps in Turkey.

Some projects operate on almost non-existent funds, while others have budgets of huge proportions. There are as many variations as there are projects. Most have community support and help from interested and skillful adults, but some operate against the grain of their community with only the efforts and commitment of the young people themselves. Some projects deal directly with issues or questions around substance abuse – perhaps by addressing risk factors (such as lack of awareness or education, for example) that increase the chance of young people abusing substances. Other projects focus on strengthening individual and community factors (protective factors) that allow young people to resist drugs. Substance abuse prevention may occur as a positive side effect.

What is Performance?
(That is, what are we talking about?)

We are using the word performance loosely to cover a wide range of expressive art forms such as dance, theatre, drama, public speaking and music. In this broad sense, performance includes public showings of final products or, the primary emphasis may be on the process of creating without deliberate consideration of an outside audience. The common thread is that performance involves a leap out of the ordinary – a deliberate choice to express something in a creative or different way. This leap may be very natural for some people, but for others, it is indeed difficult to forsake usual, safe ways of doing things for creative and challenging endeavours.

Drama gives me something that I can take with me out of the classroom or theatre, a confidence in my abilities as an actor, and a critic. This confidence gives me the ability to choose not to use drugs or alcohol without feeling pressured by others to change my mind. Kennedy, age 16

Performance – the Product

We commonly think of performance as some kind of product – the end result of long hours of rehearsing, practicing, and creating. A performance most often implies an audience of some kind that is invited to observe or perhaps even to participate. Performance can take many forms, from plays to concerts to exhibitions to talent shows.

Performance – the Process

Performance as a process may be a somewhat less familiar notion. The emphasis in this case is on the doing or creating without any intention of showing a final product publicly. Young people involved in this type of performing may be motivated by the art form's intrinsic rewards, or they may be attracted to rewards flowing as a result of the activity.

Therapies using art, music, drama or other forms of expression are common examples of performance as a process.

Why Use Performance to Combat Substance Abuse?

Performance is very captivating and beneficial to both participants and audiences. Choosing to do something in a different and creative way, to take on a role that you might not do in your ordinary life, to take a public risk by expressing yourself in a personal way often involves diligent rehearsal of complex skills, self examination and self assurance. It usually involves interpersonal skills such as working cooperatively in a group to reach a common goal, accepting others and communicating effectively. The development and practice of these characteristics along with others make for resilient youth, better able to withstand problems that can lead to substance abuse. But audiences can benefit as well, by being exposed to the accomplishments of young people, by learning more about substance abuse, and perhaps by participating in some solution building. The organization benefits through using performance to accomplish its goals and ultimately, the whole community can become a safer, more supportive environment.

PERFORMANCE

When I had a sax solo in my jazz band, it was really cool that after I practised so long, other people got to hear what I could do. This gave me a chance to show off my skill, which made me proud. *Alex, age 14*

Performance helps me to unwind and relax and it's one of the few art forms where the end result is irrelevant to me. *Laura, age 16*

What can Performance do for Young People?

Young people, when given performance opportunities that encourage creative expression can:

- grow and develop by trying new ways of doing things

  I enjoy being a part of a performance because it gives me an opportunity to get away from being myself, to meet new people and learn new things. Christine, Age 16

- practise different responses to situations that help them learn how to react creatively to future situations or problems

  When I have a problem or I feel overwhelmed by life, I find my sketchbook is an excellent way to express how I feel. The problem seems smaller once it's drawn on paper. Laura, age 16

- learn and practise the actual skills involved in their area of performance such as dancing, singing, acrobatics, juggling, design
- learn more about themselves

  I do believe that if I didn't have performing as a part of my life, I wouldn't be who I am. Jon, age 16

- learn and practise skills that are prized in the job market like creativity, communication skills and discipline

  [Performing] helps me meet new people and build the confidence in getting a new job and talking in front of people. Courtney, age 17

  It (drama) has helped me in the sense that I have become more disciplined, and I have tried to become a more dependable person, and have kept out of trouble to make sure I can do some plays. Dustin, Age 17

- meet new friends with common interests and goals
- learn how to work cooperatively with others to reach common goals

  You learn to work with everyone and you may not like everyone, but you must establish a working relationship. Natasha, age 16

- achieve a feeling of success and accomplishment (this is especially true for young people who have difficulty succeeding in traditional learning environments or who have limited opportunities for success)
- increase self esteem and self-confidence

  Since I started performing I am much more confident in front of an audience, whether I am giving a speech or even socializing. Natasha, age 16

Being active in drama plays a huge role in how I feel about myself, and what I do with my life. It's given me direction, and the confidence to go after what I want. I feel great when I'm performing, watching, and experiencing the art of theatre. Kennedy, age 16

connect with people from different age groups

develop cultural and interpersonal sensitivity

Drama helps me understand others through working with characterization. Kristen, age 17

 have fun and relieve boredom

Working on plays has given me something to do and keeps me busy in a small town like this. Amanda, age 16

experience the thrill of creative and artistic expression

I like performing because I really like being in front of an audience. I get a really good feeling when I do something funny to make somebody laugh. I like being the centre of attention so acting fits in perfectly. Its helps me express myself and I like how I can let my sense of humour come through. Jamie, age 16

achieve recognition from peers and other members of their community

Seeing the enjoyment on people's faces is a feeling so great I can't explain it. Natasha, age 16

 have access to a stable and productive activity

I like the way our band director knows how to balance fun and actually getting work done. He's really funny but we also get things accomplished. If he wasn't there to give us an activity to focus on, there'd be no point in being there. It wouldn't be possible for us to organize it ourselves. Alex, age 14

develop meaningful relationships with others including supportive adults and other role models

be role models themselves for other young people

experience and value activities that are not compatible with substance abuse

I want to be an actress, and I've chosen not to let drugs or alcohol get in the way of me achieving my dream. I choose to spend my time doing things that will help me achieve my goal, such as learning lines, developing characters and improving myself as a performer, and not use drugs or alcohol. Kennedy, age 16

Not all the above benefits may appeal to or be available for every young person involved in performing. However, even if only a few of the above benefits are realized, the result may be a more resilient young person who is able to deal with risky situations and make choices that lead to his/her desired goals.

PERFORMANCE

Why Relate Performance to Substance Abuse?

If the performance opportunities are directly related to substance abuse or social issues, there can be added benefits for the young person to:

- learn more about drugs and alcohol and identify and analyse the consequences of substance abuse

> **A Great Idea!**
> *Prevention specialists of the Alberta Alcohol and Drug Abuse Commission (Canada) often use dramatic exercises, adapted drama games and role playing to teach school children about the consequences of substance abuse. For example, classes may participate in a charade-type game that helps them identify the reasons why young people may or may not use substances.*

- learn skills to help make and stick to decisions regarding substance abuse (like refusal skills, assertiveness)
- learn how to communicate difficult thoughts and emotions through artistic expression
- identify and analyse personal problems and issues and explore individualized solutions

> **A Great Idea!**
> *The Inner City Youth Drama Association in Edmonton, Canada has found that performance is helpful for young people living on the street to deal with past issues and find solutions. Working with some of the most distressed teenagers, leaders in this association provide safe opportunities for the young people to tell their stories in a dramatic form. These stories are then woven into a collage for public presentation. Audiences that have been moved by their stories and music have included other young people in trouble and public decision makers.*

- identify and analyse community problems and issues and explore solutions
- understand the experiences of others.

Drama and performing have helped me [learn] how to stand up for myself.
Amanda, age 16

And What Else?

All these benefits can spill out into other parts of the person's life. Young people involved in performing and creative opportunities may:

- develop better overall coping skills
- experience gains in other life areas, like school work

Check this out!

"Many students find that the arts help them master academic skills. Drawing helps writing. Song and poetry make facts memorable. Drama makes history more vivid and real. Creative movement makes processes understandable. This is doubly true for the high-risk student, who often excels for the first time in an arts programme. Sometimes, the student who is not doing well in traditional academics might have an artistic talent that has not yet flowered." (Source: On-line pamphlet "Eloquent Evidence" published by the President's Committee on the Arts and the Humanities and the National Assembly of State Arts Agencies, using material published by the National Endowment for the Arts)

What About the Audience? What do they get?

For audiences, young and old, watching young people perform or present creative endeavours can:

- be very entertaining
- be educational
- be inspiring
- help them identify and analyse issues and look at solutions to their community's problems

A Great Idea!

Angaza, a theatre for change troupe in Nairobi, Kenya, creates plays with poor, abused or homeless children and teens about the problems that they are facing. The young people then present their plays to a wide audience in villages, and audience members are invited to become part of the play and act out potential solutions. Working surprisingly well despite a strong cultural norm that children are to be seen and not heard, this type of forum theatre has adult audience members participating enthusiastically, contributing positively to solutions.

PERFORMANCE

Watching a play shows you the commitment and work the actors have done to be able to perform, proving to you that if you wanted to do that, well, anything's possible. Kaitlyn, age 16

help them see the young people they know and young people in general in a positive light

inspire discussion of issues

And for the Organization?

Organizations interested in using performance as a product and/or as a process can:

transmit messages about drugs and alcohol to a variety of audiences in an entertaining and culturally relevant way

> **! A Great Idea!**
> *Eventos X Amor, a Guatemalan theatre troupe made up of young recovering drug addicts, uses culturally recognizable puppets in drug education plays for school children. They find their traditional performance approach has high acceptance levels with adults as well as children and that the humorous stories told by puppets helps minimize resistance to their messages. This type of performance has low manpower needs and is very portable. And there's the added benefit that performers develop and maintain life-long skills while contributing to their community.*

use performance to educate decision makers about young people and substances

get recognition and support for the group's causes and issues

provide performance opportunities with all the potential benefits for young people at risk of developing substance problems

contribute to the overall health of a community

use public performances as vehicles for fund-raising.

Types of Performance

The types of performance in which young people are involved are as varied
as there are projects. Here is a list of ideas for theatre and performance that
groups around the world have done and you might find appropriate for your
group. This is just a starting point for your imagination and an illustration
of the potential projects in this area. For some detailed descriptions and
more ideas, try the web sites on page 28.

Dance
- traditional/folk
- artistic
- popular/modern dance forms

Poetry
- reading
- writing
- original compositions
- traditional
- from literature

Music
- traditional/folk
- original compositions
- from existing compositions
- improvised
- singing
- playing instruments
- rapping

Puppetry
- using traditional puppets
- using created puppets
- using people as puppets

Story telling
- folk tales/traditional stories
- original stories
- from literature
- improvised

PERFORMANCE

Theatre

- **street theatre** (on the streets in the community with community members as well as some actors forming part of the audience)
- **mime**
- **travelling or touring theatre** (the performance goes to the audience, rather than the other way around)
- **participatory theatre** (at points during the performance, the audience is asked to contribute in some way – suggesting a solution, singing along, side-coaching an actor, for example)
- **forum theatre** (a particular kind of participatory theatre, when audience members are invited to come up on stage and actually act out solutions to problems posed in the performance)
- **magic**
- **clowning**
- **musical theatre**
- **skits** (brief dramatizations, they may be improvised or rehearsed)
- **political theatre**
  - on the street or in established theatres
  - using existing or commissioned scripts
  - pertaining to governments/issues
- existing scripted plays with a message that speaks to young people

---

A Great Idea!
Many youth performance groups and classes have performed modern adaptations of Shakespeare's Romeo and Juliet *to help them understand issues of race, language and religious tensions.*

- **Reader's theatre** (actors sit on stage and read their lines directly from scripts; sets are minimal (often just stools) and costume pieces are suggestive rather than complete)

Variety shows

- talent shows (allows for maximum individual participation and showcasing)
- pet/animal shows

Visual arts

- art work/painting graffiti
- photography

- use of media (e.g. video, animation, computer)
- folk art and crafts (such as pottery, sculpture, carving, masks, kites, basketry, novelties)
- design (costumes, stage, clothing, furniture, fabric, etc.)
- cartooning

Carnivals/celebrations/festivals/circuses

- Thematic (for example, awareness of issues about substance abuse)
- Celebratory/traditional
- Competitions (in drawing, dancing, music, graffiti)

Developmental drama

- role playing – (a form of practising new roles and new ways of dealing with problems)

PERFORMANCE

- theatre for job training and readiness (practising and rehearsing skills like interviewing, communication)
- improvisation of life situations
- performing positive roles (performing your life in a positive manner)

Artistic expression as therapy

- drama therapy (dramatic exercises and portrayals facilitated by a therapist as part of the treatment for young people experiencing mental health problems, substance abuse or other serious issues)
- social drama (a form of therapy for social groups. For example, when working with a family experiencing problems, members could switch roles and portray each other's feelings and experiences)
- art therapy (creation of visual art and manipulation of artistic materials as part of a treatment programme)
- music therapy (use of music, creation of music as part of a treatment programme)

Theatre in education

- dramatic exploration of events and issues for educational purposes
- public speaking/debating.

Choosing a Project

As you can see from the list above, there are many ideas for projects that use performance as a way of directly or indirectly preventing substance abuse. There are also many possibilities for creating multi-disciplinary projects that pull together two or more art forms. What your group chooses will depend upon a number of things, such as:

- the needs of your community in general (for example, if there is a very low level of awareness of substance abuse, you might want to undertake a theatre project with a goal of simply increasing awareness. However, if the community is relatively well-informed, you might consider participatory or forum theatre)
- the purpose of your group and the needs of the individual young people in your group (for example, appropriate ideas would be different for a recreational group as compared to a therapeutic group)
- the imagination, interests and abilities of members and leaders

- the composition of the target group and/or audience (for example age, gender, level of pre-existing knowledge of substance abuse, economic background, etc.)
- your financial, physical and human resources
- the existing programmes in your community (for example, there may be possibilities for networking with other groups, filling gaps that are left unfilled by them and working cooperatively with other groups)
- the level and type of community support available (from individuals, volunteers, businesses, churches and governments)
- the cultural, economic and political climate in your community.

Of course, there's something to be said for learning as you go along. However, considering the factors listed above before you settle on your choice of project may increase the effectiveness of your programme. Below is some handy advice from people who have learned a lot from their experience in using performance to help combat substance abuse.

Tips for Using Performance to Combat Substance Abuse

Getting Started:

- Starting small is not only okay, but is absolutely necessary. Performance projects can by their very nature be very small.

A Great Idea!

The All Stars Talent Show Network, New York began very small, by selling newspapers on street corners to support what they thought was a good idea – allowing disadvantaged young people to perform in Talent Shows. Through hard work and dedication, that good idea grew to its present form where the network now reaches 20,000 inner-city youngsters between the ages of 5 and 25 annually and where parallel groups have been started in other major United States cities.

- *Consider starting a performance project or group within an existing local group – seek out opinion leaders from the youth themselves.*

PERFORMANCE

> **!** *A Great Idea!*
>
> ● *In Bogota, Colombia, the UCPI (Unidad Coordinadora de Prevencion Integral) is a network linking together the 220 youth clubs that exist in the city. "Rumba Sana", a UCPI campaign to encourage young people to participate in alcohol-free activities, was developed and offered to the clubs. This promotion supports festivals, concerts, theatre, dances, poetry readings, carnivals, fiestas, mask and costume workshops and graffiti displays, all of which are alcohol-free. Each club adopts components of the programme that best suit their needs and with the resources and support from the government, youth in and around Bogota are having a great time without alcohol.*

∴ Performance as a part of a treatment or rehabilitation process is an excellent way to get started.

> **!** *A Great Idea!*
>
> ● *AADAC (Alberta Alcohol and Drug Abuse Commission) Youth Services in Edmonton, Canada undertook a video project with a group of teenagers in a residential programme for young people with mental health concerns. This video chronicled the downward spiral of a fictitious teenager who had abused drugs. The residents worked very hard on this programme, researching information on substance abuse, long and short-term effects of drugs, as well as available treatment programmes.*

∴ Working with young people who already know each other can be valuable (they don't have to get to know each other or learn to trust each other from scratch).
∴ Stay calm and don't get discouraged if you don't see miracles (or even your expected results) at the beginning.
∴ Seek out help from local artists and organizations – you can find some amazing allies and help in this corner.

> **!** *Check this out!*
>
> ● *Coming Up Taller is a United States government programme of recognition for exemplary projects involving young people and the arts. In their report (which can be found on-line), they describe over 250 projects and sing the praises of "the men and women who share their skills as they help to shape the talents of children and youth and tap their hidden potentials. These dedicated individuals, often working long hours for little pay, are educators, social workers, playwrights, actors, poets, videographers, museum curators, dancers, musicians, muralists, scholars and librarians."* (Source: On-line report "Coming Up Taller" published by the President's Committee on the Arts and the Humanities)

And About the Performance:

⫶ The most effective performances are specific to their target communities.

⫶ Be imaginative and persistent when looking for content to perform especially when you're looking for stories to tell or dramatize. You can find stories by:

  ⫶ talking to people informally or formally (especially if they are in your target group)

  ⫶ talking a walk through neighbourhoods

  ⫶ looking at photographs, newspapers, pamphlets, scripts, poetry, magazines, literature, movies

  ⫶ adapting folk tales and traditional stories

  ⫶ visiting art galleries, museums, archives and other public places

⫶ Don't let lack of space bog you down – use what's available. You can have a stage anywhere. Performance can happen in many places – by the side of a building, in a shopping mall, on the street, in a classroom, in the subway, in parks, in community centres, in parking lots, in vacant lots.

PERFORMANCE

> *A Great Idea!*
>
> *The Society for Theatre Education for People (STEP) in New Delhi, India uses street theatre to educate large groups of poor people about alcohol addiction and treatment facilities. Young people who have dropped out of school from the target communities are the performers, making their dramatisations more relevant for the audience and increasing their acceptance. The costs and logistics of the productions are minimal for this highly mobile show – there are no cumbersome set pieces, lighting or space requirements. This type of theatre has high visibility in the community and audiences flock to their performances.*

⫶ Use lots of volunteers in your projects and encourage their active participation in many aspects of the performance.

> *A Great Idea!*
>
> *For every talent show they run, the All Stars Network operates with an army of approximately 100 volunteers. All their fund-raising efforts are person to person with volunteers programmes sponsored by the All Stars Project made possible through the generosity of more than 30,000 donors and hundreds of volunteers annually.*

⫶ Performance about social issues is more effective if you carefully plan the build up to the event and then do a follow-up activity.

> **A Great Idea!**
> *STEP, the Society for Theatre Education of the People in New Delhi, India makes it a point to talk with young people in each slum community they perform in. STEP gets a better idea of their problems and concerns and incorporates these into the story it develops for its street plays. Not only does this ensure that young people in the community are truly involved in the process, it also ensures that the stories STEP tells are more believable.*

> **A Great Idea!**
> *Concrete Theatre in Canada is a professional theatre company that performs participatory theatre about issues that young people may be facing, such as choices around substance abuse. Often performed in schools, the shows include a number of opportunities for student participation during the performance, pre-and post show educational activities and talkback sessions. Teachers are given pre- and post-performance materials to use in their classrooms as well as support for their use.*

- Don't let the pressing demands of an end-product overshadow the importance of the process of creating the performance. You can do this by building in lots of debriefing time and setting the show date well after rehearsal and development is underway.
- When dealing with emotional subjects, it is important to let the people in the group get to know each other slowly so they can develop trust and a sense of working together.

> **A Great Idea!**
> *Many groups, especially those using theatre as their performance choice, use Ice Breakers (simple physical exercises that involve working with one or several partners) and warm-up activities to help actors get to know each other so they can feel comfortable while working on their performance.*

- Before, during and after performing, young actors should have an opportunity to talk about their experiences with each other.

- When thinking about costumes, props, etc. creativity is important – it will save you money and keep the performance interesting.

> *A Great Idea!*
>
> ● *The costumes used by the actors in STEP of India are simple black outfits – costumes worn by some of the traditional performers in this country. They use minimal props or set pieces; their stage is simply a rug set out on the ground. They rely successfully on the imagination of the actors and the audience to create their captivating and educational dramatic pieces.*

Don't be discouraged if you have small audiences. No matter how small the audience, the performance is still important to them.

Promoting Events:

Use posters/banners in schools and colleges to attract young people.

Put posters, etc. at places where you can find your intended audience.

Use enticing giveaways to attract people/audiences.

> *A Great Idea!*
>
> ● *Again, take STEP as an example. Often, they give out crayons and coloured pens to the children in their target community. Actors draw attention by playing a hand drum and calling people out of their houses to come and watch the show. Sometimes, they even give out things like pinwheels and paper boats to the kids. The idea is that if the kids come running to see the show, the adults can not be far behind!*

Work closely with groups of intended audiences. Involving them in the process of performance will increase your relevance for them, their interest in your project and the likelihood they will attend and bring others.

Enlist the support of the media – newspapers, radio, TV. Perhaps your event has a human-interest element to it that will be attractive to the media.

PERFORMANCE

Living with a Limited Budget:

∴ Use minimal, creative costuming. Newspapers, tin foil, gunny sacks and even leaves can be used to create amazing costumes.
∴ Use people to represent objects, set pieces.
∴ If you build set pieces, start your collection with some basics (like doorframes, cubes, stairs sets, etc.) that can be altered with paint, paper and or lighting. Something simple, like a cube, can be used for many different things – a chair, a table, dice, and a building block.

General Advice:

∴ Think wide, creative, crazy, and open-minded!
∴ Allow young people to have freedom of expression so they will be able to fully participate and work toward realizing their dreams.
∴ Be relevant to your target group by being visible and available – go to where they are.
∴ Stay open to ideas and new people – welcome new people into your group.

Involvement of Youth

The potential for young people to be involved in performance projects is vast. However, young people won't necessarily flock to the opportunities presented to them. The tips below may be helpful in generating ideas for you to ensure that young people become involved in a meaningful way. We can encourage the involvement of young people by:

∴ inviting them on an individual basis to participate in the activities
∴ showing off their talents
∴ supporting their peer groups and their friends
∴ creating a 'safe' and inviting place for them to express their ideas, try out new skills, meet new people, be themselves
∴ asking for and trying out their input and ideas for projects
∴ choosing projects that are inviting to them and their families
∴ including them in a variety of ways in the project
∴ recruitment of other young people
∴ playwriting
∴ fund-raising
∴ choreography
∴ creating costumes
∴ stage managing

- running lights and sound
- producing, directing
- designing flyers and posters
- creating plays, music and poems
- designing make-up
- building sets
- cooking food for the show
- making a video of the performance

! A Great Idea!

The All Stars Talent Show Network is definitely a success story in terms of youth involvement – both short and long term. Focusing on young people from the most disadvantaged areas in American cities such as New York, they operate from a very broad meaning of performance as they conduct their yearly season of "everyone-gets-in" auditions, performance workshops and talent shows. In addition to singing, rapping, dancing and acting onstage for the Talent Shows, young people promote the All Stars in their communities. They are the ticket sellers, the stagehands, the sound and light crews, the ushers and the security team. Everyone is performing as part of the whole event, making a contribution to themselves and their communities. Retention of youth is high in this unique programme as young people return year after year, many of them assuming leadership positions.

- creating leadership opportunities in the project for young people
- acknowledging and honouring their active participation (especially "backstage" input)
- ensuring there are flexible rules to join the group provisions
- networking with existing organizations where young people are already there – schools, colleges, clubs, teams, residences, etc.
- keeping in contact with them through newsletters, internet, phone calls
- providing other opportunities for socializing along with the performance
- giving them opportunities to share their ideas and problems, giving them a voice and space to express their wishes and dreams
- involving their existing leaders in the programme
- expanding their understanding of their world through cultural and religious exchanges, field trips to hospices, group homes and other communities
- expanding their artistic knowledge and experience through fieldtrips to art exhibitions, performances, concerts, etc.

PERFORMANCE

∴ not being afraid to have high expectations for the young people in terms of their behaviour. Some basic ground rules include: coming to rehearsals, workshops, performances, etc. free of substances, being on time, etc. You might want to negotiate these expectations with the young people and even draw up contracts.

∴ Providing food and other necessities is sometimes the first step to getting the young people involved.

A Great Idea!

The Inner City Drama Association (ICDA) in Edmonton, Canada provided food as incentive, and in many cases as necessary, for its members. Responding to the needs of the young people in the drama group, ICDA at one time provided housing and now runs a comprehensive school for young people living in the inner city.

Sources and Resources

Written Materials:

Here are some written materials you might find helpful.

- Boal, Augusto, **Theatre of the Oppressed**, (translated by C. A. and M. L. McBride), New York: Urizen Books, 1977
  This is Augusto Boal's (the internationally-renowned Brazilian theatre maker and political activist) first book on using theatre to transform society. It has been translated into at least 25 languages and his techniques are used throughout the world.

- Boal, Augusto, **Games for Actors and Non-Actors**, (translated by Adrian Jackson) London and New York: Routlage, 1992. (Also available in French)
  This book outlines games, methods and techniques that can be used with performers and is appropriate for anyone interested in using theatre as a force for social and political change.

- Schutzman, Mady and Cohen-Cruz, Jan, eds., **Playing Boal: Theatre**, **Therapy**, **Activism**, London and New York: Routlage, 1994.
  This book consists of individual chapters describing how Boal's work has been adapted by groups throughout the world.

- Hodgson, John, ed., **The Uses of Drama: Acting as a Social and Educational Force**, London: Eyre Methuen Ltd., 1972
  This book is a collection of articles on how drama can be used to educate individuals and cause social change.

PERFORMANCE

Web Sites

Performance groups

∷ Inner City Youth Development Association
http://www.innercityyouth.org/

∷ All Stars Talent Show Network
http://www.allstars.org/allstars.htm

Ideas for Performance Projects

∷ Coming Up Taller Awards
http://www.cominguptaller.org/inside.html
This American web page describes in some detail over 350 unique performance projects that exist in the United States for young people. It also includes additional information on the benefits of performance for young people and links to other sites.

∷ Drug & Alcohol Response Teams Main Page
http://www.adfq.org/darts.html#Home
This Australian web page describes a number of possible projects for combating drug and alcohol abuse, including some imaginative ideas for using performance.

Special Acknowledgements

Special thanks to the following people who contributed to the development of this text:

- Carolyn Howrath, Concrete Theatre in Edmonton, Canada
- Employees of AADAC who contributed to this project, especially Bernice Osinchuk, Carol Cameron, Paddy Meade and Ramon Flores
- Keith Ewasiuk, drama teacher at Beaumont High School and the students in his drama classes
- Joe Cloutier, Inner City Youth Drama Association
- Jan Selman, Chair, University of Alberta Department of Drama

PERFORMANCE